I0411331

The Peace of Gaza

Text Copyright © 2012 by Stephen Paul West

Cover Design Copyright © 2012 by Stephen Paul West

Visit the Author at: **www.StephenPaulWest.com**

LIBRARY OF CONGRESS CATALOGING-IN-PUBLICATION DATA

West, Stephen Paul
The Peace of Gaza / Stephen Paul West
p. cm.

● ● ● ●

Summary: An alternate history twenty-years from today. Peace dwells in Gaza City. In this history three participants of the Gaza Strip discover that peace comes only with sacrifice.

ISBN-13: 978-1481068345

ISBN-10: 1481068342

Shocking Press Publications

Dedication

I dedicate this story to peace.

Sometimes the world must do something new and powerful to change constant and protracted war.

My story is an alternate history. Twenty years from today.

I must point out that much of the Islamic dialogue used in this story are direct quotes from Osama Bin Laden and various imam's still living in Gaza at this moment. I didn't wish to dilute the message of extremists in the slightest.

In spite of the difficulties, this short story dares to imagine a history that is free of war in the Gaza Strip.

Peace in the City of Gaza

Hidden Knowledge

CHAPTER 1

A Wintry Plaza Meeting

People say I am beautiful, so I know my mother is a rare beauty. Still, she prefers to be the widow of a father I never met, than to remarry any man still living upon earth. This is strange to me. This is my mother.

So cold. So very cold. Tears splash easily over my lashes.

I don't know why I come to this place. It makes me shiver even on a warm day. However, today is freezing, even without the memories. Gaza City has dipped into a record low temperature. *Brrr.* The people are all at home where it is warm. I walk alone.

Oops. Almost alone. I see two older men walking about. They have yet to noticed me.

The beautiful plaza sits in steel-grey cold. Everything here is new except for a single ancient olive tree. It is a survivor, and the gardeners made no attempt to protect it from the freeze. The bushes are tied with sheets to protect against the frost. I like the way the sheets pop and snap in the billowing wind. The white-painted fountains are closed and waterless for the winter. The harsh wind swirls dry leaves in scratchy, tiny whirlwinds in these silent, dry fountains. Still, this place is lovely even in the cold. Bereft of people it is even lovelier. My heart prefers the stony solitude. The wind cuts icy, carried from snowy Europe to blow frosty across the Mediterranean. But none of this is what stabs my inner soul with frigid melancholy.

Indeed, my tears fall so icy that they burn my face as they evaporate. Yes, it is an unusual day in Gaza City, but not just for the cold. Today is the anniversary of my father's death.

My feet touch right at the very heart of the long dead beast that killed my father. It is stupid for me to come to this place. My mother would cry and scold me as if I were a child — but I must come to this place sometimes. I stand upon the same place, which birthed the Qassam missiles that smashed into my parent's small apartment twenty years ago. Missiles that murdered my father, him having never seen me.

I, at least, get to see him from time to time in old

photos. I smile down at his unmoving, unblinking face. Sometimes I hear my mother still weep over these old photos. My father must have been a very good husband because my mother never remarried — and the lines of her face are much fairer than mine.

She is still young in today's world. A shapely forty-three, but like an old bobeshi, I sometimes hear her talking to God on the back porch of our sea-side apartment.

"God," says she, "I want to thank you for the wonderful years You gave me with Yosef. I miss him, but I am also grateful for finding such love when most women never touch any such thing as I had. I still feel love yet in my heartbeat. May Maya know and feel her father's love even now. Thank You."

With many other words she thanks God for having found great love in her life. I was embarrassed of her prayers until my best friend Fatima came to sleep over. I knew Fatima's parents loved her very much. I always like her house because she has both parents. I guess I like just seeing a dad around — even if not my own.

We were twelve, and Fatima heard my mother pray such a thing at the dawn hours of morning. My mother went out on the porch, as I supposed she felt it was very private. The walls of the open porch simply carried even a whisper up into my open bedroom window.

I was going to apologize for my mother, but Fatima wept and wept at the prayer. It was then I realized my mother had something true. And this was something so rare that my twelve year old girlfriend should weep for hours. I learned so much that morning. Fatima still cannot tell me of that day without shedding tears. I love Fatima. I love my mother. And yes, I love a father I never met. I know he loved me before I was born.

So, I come to this place because…well, it is strange because this is the very place of the missile base that killed my father.

The week my mother prayed, and Fatima cried, I went and searched for my father. I started small. I typed in the day he died, and the words '*missiles*' and '*gaza*'. A simple search of a simple child. The very first result was a twenty year old BBC article. It reported that Gaza extremists shot eight thousand six hundred missiles into Israel, most of them during '*truce times*'. I felt as if every single one of those projectiles of hate and bigotry hit my father. That moment changed me into a seeker of truth.

Eight thousand six hundred missiles shot during '*truce*'?

I laugh aloud at this absurdity. I take a quick glance at the other two visitors in the cold. Neither of them noticed my escaping laughter.

If that many missiles are '*truce*' I wondered what war would be by comparison. A nuclear bomb? Ridiculous.

This absurd fact made me do a lot of research on the missiles — a lot. I eventually came to realize that I was actually searching for the exact place that launched the exact rocket that killed my father. I didn't understand this when I started my study.

Momma, my pretty Ima, did not approve. She said I should let the memory of the dead be a blessing. '*What about life?*' my mother always says. And like a blessing, Gaza became so peaceful that even she moved here eventually. I personally think she also wants to find the place that took away her true love. We are attracted to what hurts us most.

I realize momma was right. I was…am…obsessive in my search. I tried several times just to forget it. My fingers hesitate over the keyboard, and I type a search anyway. Yes, I am compulsive. I cannot let go. Perhaps when I find out all there is to know, my heart will find tranquility.

My father died at 9:17a.m. By 9:30a.m. this base was a smoking crater. Thirteen minutes between a little girl knowing her father, and a little girl raised alone by her mother. I learned that this spot – somewhere below my feet – lays the very location that brought such tragedy to my Ima and me.

So what if tears burn icy cold upon my cheek? I am Maya, the daughter of my mother. I feel love in my heartbeat, as well.

I am glad the plaza is empty except for a Muslim

gentleman standing over by the fountain.

Oh, and a single other guard I can tell was a soldier once upon a time. It is just us three all wandering about this spacious and lovely plaza. Only I know that a horrible missile base lay long buried beneath our feet.

I alone know the secret of being here.

The security-soldier disappears as he paces about the plaza. He just turned behind the immaculately groomed bushes covered with fluttering sheets. I still hear his rough accent talking to his wife. He is obviously a former American who married an Israeli woman. Many of these GIs stayed after the world's armies intervened in Gaza. I can tell soldiers. He walks like a soldier – and even though he speaks sweetly to his wife – he also speaks like a soldier. All solutions, all the time. Still, it is sweet he tries to speak Hebrew. He is really bad at it too! Certainly, his wife speaks English, but this middle-aged soldier tries to please her. That is sweet. My papa would have certainly tried the same thing if he had been American.

The two men are clueless to the tears on my cheeks. A woman would notice them from across three piazzas larger than this wide square. These oafish men? They would not see them if I should wipe them on their chests. Men don't see such things.

● ● ● ●

I see the stupid Zionist girl profane the graves of my brothers. Had Allah not called me away to do the bidding of Hamas and get the guidance coordinates, I too, would have been turned to ashes and splinters of bones upon this very spot. The stupid girl wanders about as if not a single care in the world. She offends my eyes. Jewess usurper. She steps upon the graves of the holy with her filthy, infidel feet.

I am filled with rage. Twenty years of rage! No, a thousand times more. I am the rage of every Jihadist forced from this place. We would still be fighting the Jews from here if the Zion loyalist had not sent us back to the homes of our fathers.

Egypt? Feh! I am only a son of Egypt in memory. My place, by the choice of Allah, is this Gaza land. I alone have returned to strike the blow of memory.

Forced repatriation! It offends me.

United Nation kafirs!

In my day, this place was teeming with the voices of the people — proud to watch my brethren and I put a Qassam stick into the eye of Tel Aviv. Now, the criers of the mosques here are timid. As if they are ashamed of the only true God, and his prophet Mohammad (peace be upon him). I alone remember this place when the battle fought fierce upon this sacred soil. Where are those who should join me? Absent. Either out of death, or out of damnable cowardice.

7

I alone am the last true son of Gaza.

I alone know the secret of being here.

The city glitters in white and decadence. The Jews have made it as a pearl of the Mediterranean instead of the battle ground of al-Badr al-Abyah al-Mutawassi. All the merchants and vile tourists walk about this city as if made of gold. They forget the graves of all Allah's martyrs when we had this place. If the world had given us this much money, we might have built just as much decadent beauty — but first we would have driven the cursed Jews from our Holy land. Guns and missiles before these polished stones and brazen white paint.

Fight those who believe not in Allah nor the Last Day, fight those who hold that forbidden which hath been forbidden by Allah and His Messenger, nor acknowledge the religion of Truth. Even if they are of the People of the Book, until they pay the Jizya with willing submission, and feel themselves subdued.

I am proud I was Hamas then. I am proud I am Hamas today. I am proud I hate the Zionist so much. The Muslims in this city are fat and lazy. They are reprobates who are drunk on foreign money and the cleanliness of the city streets. A few rats would educate them best. The cowards are willing to live in peace besides Jews and Christians. It offends Allah and it offends me as His messenger.

Ah, kafir! The cold makes this plaza empty. How shall I

send my message of vengeance? A single stupid girl? That security man pacing around this place? He does not fool me. He will come soon and check my papers. I will be as docile as a dove. I have family and business reasons to be here. My papers are legal. My heart he cannot read, as Allah will conceal my plans to shed blood for His glory. My smile is so insipid as to charm a cobra. This bumbling guard shall be blind.

Perhaps a single girl with beguiling beauty is even a better message? The world will not forget the image of that Jew girl bleeding on these too polished stones.

She is too pretty and her face offends me in uncovered lack of virtue. All the better for the world to see the error of what was done here. My name shall be remembered as a martyr.

Ah, here comes that military jackal.

●　●　●　●

"Just a second, Sweetie."

I hate switching to English on my wife, but the guy at the corner looks kinda strange. I can barely speak Hebrew when I'm fully focused, but now I'm distracted entirely.

I hang up the phone and walk straight over to the guy like we are old friends. I once had a hostage negotiator tell me I should always approach suspects from an *obtuse angle* – whatever the hell that is – so I'm perceived as friendly.

Well, in my business I don't have time for friendly '*obtuse*'. It might have been good advice for a hostage negotiator. Unfortunately, life is often much more direct for men like me. Sure, I developed the skills for being '*obtuse*'. I also mastered the art of being direct and acute. Maybe this is what I'm best at. I dunno.

He gives me a nod as I walk over.

"Hello." My tone is authoritative. I am a guard after all.

"Hello, my friend." His greeting is too relaxed.

I smile disarmingly at him in return.

Today I'm a little distracted. I feel outside of my own head just being in this place. I stood here twenty years ago as a much younger and stronger soldier. Now, the nostalgia is making me cloudy. Hell, I'm even a little bit depressed standing on these stones. I miss being with my wife instead. I think I'll retire the end of this year. I've stayed too long in this game.

I shake my head a little to get back into the present.

This guy just isn't right. Sure, maybe I picked him out because it's slim pickings today. It's just him, myself and that pretty young gal with those tears in her eyes. I bet some guy is going to regret breaking her heart. It'll take about two seconds for her to find another boyfriend, that's for sure.

Naw. Even if this plaza were thumping with a parade, this guy would have brought my attention. Man, I'm so glad this is rare now-a-days. God, when was the last time I had this feeling? Maybe eight, nine years ago? I dunno. People sure bitched about the expulsion of the Gaza strip at first, but it turned a shithole into a much nicer place. No more war. That feels good to me. I'm tired of hate. I'm tired of humanity to be honest. I hardly ever worry about these kind of checks anymore.

I wonder what my wife is making for dinner? I hope there is some hot chocolate. I'm fricken' freezin'

"Good morning. Cold, huh? Do you have a light?"

I don't even bother to present a cigarette. Hell, I don't even smoke. We both know this is just a polite way for me to have him frisk himself. Sometimes I hate my job. Sometimes I hate being really, really good at it.

"Let me see." He pats his pockets. He is entirely too thorough. He must have done this a time or two. He knows if he is too brief than I will most definitely search him myself. He must be old Mujahideen. These guys used to be serious business years ago. All retired now. I should join them.

He even turns when he checks his back pockets, so I can see clearly. Yeah, this poor guy has been hassled many a time at security check-points. The only place left is maybe a knife in his shoes, or something under his koufiyya. I glance at the turban. It fits tightly with a low profile and no lumps. It looks safe. It's been like ten years since there has been any terrorist violence in the entire Gaza strip. Even petty crime is low.

"That's okay. I'll get a light later." I cock my head and smile a thin smile. This guy doesn't even flinch when I raise my arms and blow into my hands to warm them up. I know he can see my pistol. I'm deliberate about this '*obtuse*' display. Nothing. Nada. His eyes are way too casual. He is even cooler than this frigid weather.

I'm done scanning him over. He certainly doesn't have a weapon on him. It's too damned cold to hassle this guy anyway. We both can tell I am a split second away from checking his papers and running his name.

He smiles at me, knowing he would pass the check.

I let it go.

"Well, don't stay out here forever in the cold. You might freeze." I puff in my hands to demonstrate how cold it is. Steam actually escapes from between my fingers.

"It is refreshing to me. I am rather enjoying the sting of the air."

This is the anniversary.

The anniversary of the knife-edge of World War III.

I don't like anybody out today. People should be at home reflecting how incredibly close we came to erasing everything. I suppose maybe people just don't know.

I know.

I'm standing on the very spot, now buried under these

paving stones, which would have birthed the end of humanity. This is a horrid spot, forgotten in time.

Now, a very lovely plaza masks the lurking evil beneath our feet.

I alone know the secret of being here.

I'm one of the few people who know that a thick layer of Baryte concrete hides the fallout beneath this exquisite place. It amazes me that the horror of humanity can be so cleverly concealed.

In the past, protests sprang up on this anniversary. At first, the protests of the Repatriation Day were angry and sometimes violent. A few years later, nothing. Jobs, money and a beautiful city sure go a long way from turning a hell-scape into a nice place to live. Nobody protests any more. Even the hippies have moved on to the Syrian and Lebanon borders. Those are still hotbeds of crazy and hate.

Huh? Suddenly I'm glad I pulled this shit-inspection duty. I could be standing watch along the Syrian border.

Gaza strip has been peaceful for twenty years — but, this peace was birthed from the very heart of the dragon. I should know. I was the one who lazed the evil heart straight to hell.

"Well, make sure you find shelter before dark."

"Yes, yes." He waves his hand at me and turns his face. I can tell he just wants me to mind my own business.

I feel like reminding him about the prohibition on anniversary day protests, but I'll admit I would just be provoking this guy. Being a dick isn't in the best interest of peace. I ignore his dismissive attitude and give another thin smile. Strangely, I find a little comfort knowing I'm talking to a guy who most likely saw the same shit as me — but obviously from the other end.

"I'll be around the plaza if you have any questions."

"Thank you. I might stay around and see if it snows. I've never seen snow."

I nod my head. It's a good idea. I implied my goodbye already, but I'm not feeling like wandering around this frozen, barren square any longer. I stand here stupidly chatting with this old Mujahideen. I'm turning into one of those soft old nostalgic ex-soldiers. Yep. Time to retire.

I might check on the crying girl in a bit once she settles down. I'm no good with tears.

I haven't seen snow in many years myself. Gaza City would be magnificent covered in snow. Good idea. I'll take some pictures if this happens.

● ● ● ●

CHAPTER 2

The Sword of Burning Heaven

I watch the two men talking.

They act like they are old friends. Even a few smiles and chuckles. I see the Arab man pat his pockets for a match. I don't know why we do that when we know we don't have matches; as if the mere exercise will magically put matches in our pockets.

Well, actually I realize we do that to demonstrate to the other person we are not withholding anything. We pat to show we are not hiding matches. People hide so much, it is only natural everybody is suspicious about mere matches.

And really, even in Israel nobody smokes anymore.

I look over at the two middle aged men. I realize they both have the look of men who smoke to make a haze of their memories. The patting ceases and they move onto another subject of more interest. No cigarettes were discovered.

I lose interest in the pair, and would prefer to be left alone anyway. The sheets tied around the topiary interest me.

I sniff away my tears for about the hundredth time since I got here this morning. Brrr. A wet face is not a happy face in this stinging wind.

Besides my bottom is getting very cold sitting on this low wall. I would stretch and rub some warmth back into my backside, but decorum has taught me that men easily detect such overt feminine actions, and male eyes cannot help but turn and watch. I am too shy for that.

Again, I laugh at my absurd ways. Nobody has EVER touched my bottom but me. And the mere thought of those men perchance noticing me rub it warm, makes me so embarrassed I want to run away. I am old enough to think about finding a boyfriend, but the University keeps me too busy. And, truthfully, I am too shy for love.

I think perhaps at nineteen that I am still too young to sleep with a man. At any rate, I make myself very small and slip away behind the blowing sheets tied around the landscaping. I know the men have not noticed because I peek at them once I am safely hid. They are still gossiping like old women.

"And men complain that women are chatty!" I whisper out loud. I take a moment to really rub my poor frozen cheeks. They are numb! I never knew that cold could freeze your tuchis solid!

I peek out from behind the sheets once again. I'm afraid my rubbing might have magically transmitted something sexually to the men. It is stupid I know. However, I am grateful both men just jabber away. My shocking behavior has not been transmitted like a radio wave. *Pshew.* Those two talk and talk!

"Yentes!" I tease out loud in a moment of naughtiness.

Imale says I am too smart and sassy for my own good. My brains scare away half the boys and my sassy mouth scares away the other half of the boys.

"Yes," I tell her then. "A woman with brains does scare away boys. But men? Real men want a smart girl! My brains shall bring a real *MAN*."

Then my mother laughs and pats my face. Sometimes she kisses my forehead and calls me '*clever girl*' or even '*cheeky*' if she wishes to sound British. I do love my Ima. She is the cheeky one!

It is true that my brains let me find the birth-place of the monster that killed my father. So perhaps my mother is right. I am too smart. Is this a sin? At any rate, I managed to break my own heart with my endless brainy-snooping.

8,600 Rockets. That's the number of rockets fired on Israel over ten years of '*truce*'. It is this absurd number that made me search. It is the number that still shocks me every morning. No wonder why the world came in with all the militaries and took over this tiny strip. They sent all the refugees home. Paid people to go home and buy houses. My, how the refugees hated it. Egypt too. But, it has been peace ever since then though. Sinai is guarded by the U.N. I've never even seen a rocket — well, except the one I must have heard when I was still inside my mother's womb. You know, one of the 8,600 that killed my papa.

It was *NOT* easy to figure out all the pieces. Until I studied vectors in school I lacked ability to calculate it all. Then I needed to learn that the range of the rockets increased over time. Perhaps this insanity might have continued until a nuclear missile was used. Then what? Judgment day for everybody.

But when a person such as myself becomes obsessed, then no detail is too small. Great is my obsession in finding everything out about my father's death. If a mere pebble had been found in his pocket, I would have it analyzed by a scientist — and I honestly would remember every detail of the results. My mind is my trap. Finding the reason for my father's death is the only escape.

So? I remember? Is that a sin? My mind is photographic. It possesses me. Maybe makes me a little crazy.

Details? I have thousands in my mind, but not a single reason why. A thousand points of data, and not a single point of understanding.

I know the original Qassam rockets had a range of about 10 km (6.2 mi) but more advanced rockets, including versions of the old Soviet Katyusha, hit Israeli targets 40 km (25 mi) from Gaza. I plotted the range of all kinds of missiles in big circles I drew, in true old-school style, using a compass on printed maps.

Who sold terrorist better and better missiles anyway?

Nothing had the range to hit my parents — except the one missile that did hit them.

One day, I found an old photo from a news archive and I saw my destroyed home. Like treasure my eyes spied a piece of fin on the balcony. I researched until I found the exact missile type.

I am choking on my sobbing again. I must push the details away.

This missile was very important information for me to learn in my searching.

I use the back of my hand to dry away the new batch of tears.

"Why should the world sudden jump into such a long war?" I say this behind the bushes in deep thought. "A moment of terror like never before would change the will of the world."

I tip my head in reflection at my own words. I am not breathing any longer and the steam just rolls out from my open lips and dances before my eyes. It is rather beautiful. It is like my soul is dancing before my very eyes. I smile at the cold for the first time.

I slip away from the two men by cautiously darting from sheet to sheet and foliage to foliage. I don't know why I'm being so cautious like a gazelle.

I guess because the cold makes my breath to steam, it is as if my soul is exposed. I'm too shy for that.

I must hide.

● ● ● ●

Ah! Where did that girl go?

This jackal continues to talk with me as if I am an old friend. He might have been a good soldier years ago, but the endless peace has made him stupid.

I smile into his face. The man is reminiscing about the old Gaza Strip. He most certainly violated holy Muslim lands to dare and fight right here in Gaza. He knows too much about the land and battle to be a simple guard. He might have even fought me personally. It makes me ill, but I smile and laugh.

"I too enjoy seeing my family here in Gaza. I am certain your wife shall have hot cocoa waiting. My Abba made me cocoa once as a child. It was cold that day – but not like this. Perhaps my ears shall fall off."

We both laugh at my remark. He has forgotten I am Hamas. I am the fox and he is the mere hen.

"So your family has claim to Gaza then?"

I can see he suddenly realizes his innocent question is offensive. As it should be. I do not let my revulsion show in the slightest.

"On my mother's side, yes. But, my father was Egyptian. So, I was sold into Egypt."

The American-Jew soldier shifts uncomfortably. My honest answer has pricked his heart.

"Sold? That is the harshest of views. If that had not occurred, there would be war here to this very day. Isn't this wonderful plaza better than lingering war? No more dead kids."

"Yes of course." I lie.

No! No! No! My heart screams the words of Umar al-Khattib when that great Imam heard the Messenger of Allah (may peace be upon him) saying: I will expel the Jews and Christians from the Arabian Peninsula and will not leave any but Muslim.

Does this vile American guard think I have forgotten my vows to my religion? The religion of Peace and Truth. No! I have not forgotten.

Lingering war? I would choose a million years of war

21

before allowing even a single Jew to build anything in holy Islamic lands.

"Well," says the guard, "I saw a thousand memories just flash in your face. I know the repatriation was difficult as first, but it did work. It brought much needed peace. Not just for the Israeli people – many of whom are Muslim themselves – but for the children of Palestine as well. Certainly, old soldiers like us can remember the mutual wreckage and kids being killed. It was horrible."

This infidel *PREACHES* at me!

"Yes, but it was difficult returning to our homelands. It certainly was not fair."

Not fair. I am using American jingo. Fair is what they think they give. The Muslim world today is faced with tyranny and injustice. Indeed, oppression and hardship is not just limited to the Muslim world, rather many non-Muslim are subject to oppression at the hands of the United Nations and the Zionists. All who care can only be saddened and hurt by the pain and suffering that accompanies so many faces. Islam has allowed Jihad as a means to prevent oppression, yet the Muslims have forgotten this for too long.

"I see your point." Now it is the GI soldier lying to me.

"Humm," I grunt as if considering his words carefully. It only encourages him to lie to me even more boldly.

"The refugees," says he, "were paid to relocate; those

with proven lineage to Gaza strip were given full citizenship. It worked. Perhaps it even stopped the world's end from nuclear war."

At the mention of the sword of Allah, I unfortunately glance fully into his face. Even the devil has his prophets and I have found one in this soldier. Ah, my martyrdom will even have more honor. I was foolish and misjudged my adversary. I must even be more clever than normal.

"End of the world? We have no such doctrine in my religion of peace."

"Really? No Qur'an text of the End of the World?" The guard tilts his head. I have told an ignorant lie. I have raised his suspicion. I can see he no longer likes me at all. A moment ago, I was an old Mujahideen friend. He felt kinship with me for both having seen this place in battle twenty years ago. Now, I have stupidly awoken his suspicion.

"Well," I recover, as if remembering something, "Islam speaks of the Judgment Day, but that is a mere metaphor."

Too late. I cannot fix my error. I saw the guard's eyes narrow. I am not a fox. I am unworthy to join those who have gone before me as martyrs. I must redeem myself quickly.

"Perhaps. But I was here when the war climbed endlessly to the very summit of insanity. Yeah, nuclear. Not a metaphoric 'End of the World'... I mean nuclear. At any rate, I can tell you that for the last twenty years Gaza has grown more and more peaceful. Everybody is happy. Atheist, Jew, Christian and Muslim." He gestures around the splendid city while he stresses the word Muslim.

Perhaps some backsliding reprobates who claim to be Muslim are happy. True believers reject such devil-spawned lies. This is why Muslims can NEVER be friends to unbelievers.

O ye who believe! Take not for friends unbelievers rather than believers: Do ye wish to offer Allah an open proof against yourselves?

"In the end it does not really matter anymore." I gesture around at the empty plaza in imitation. "The people have forgotten and become fat and lazy. The anniversary is forgotten."

"As it should. You know that protests are prohibited today?"

So my old friend is back to being my old enemy. He is a serpent.

"What's to protest? I'm just an old man sitting on a cold stone wall, remembering what this place looked like only in my forgotten memory."

"This place?"

I can tell I said too much. This infidel American is perhaps also remembering what this place looked like. Is it possible his eyes saw the same moment of time as mine? He is old enough. Did he see the missiles? Did he see the sword of

Allah itself? I doubt this could be possible, but I must be as sneaky as a stray dog.

"I mean the sea and the beach. This city as it grew into this beautiful place. Much enjoyed by your American tourists no?"

"I'm no tourist."

"Ah, and here is where we are different. I am only a tourist." I smile my insipid smile again. I am charming to this scaly cobra. Killing an American-Jew soldier is perhaps even as good as killing a hundred Jews. My smile becomes very sincere indeed.

He studies me for a moment, and his eye grows ill and dismissive. I am nothing but a worm to him. He nods his dismissal without a word.

At last that idiot security pig wanders off.

He thinks to threaten me with his gun? I myself buried mortars near that olive tree. I bet they are still waiting for me. Twenty years will just make them all more impatient to unleash their fury. If they blow me into paradise this is Allah's will.

Ah, where did that stupid woman go? She wanders about this land as if it were hers! The whole of historic Palestine is Islamic land and holy only for Muslims. Israel is but an occupier and it my duty to fight these interlopers. My imam taught me well: If then any one transgresses the prohibition against you, transgress ye likewise against him. But fear Allah, and know that Allah is with those who restrain themselves.

At this memory, I dare to say a prayer that has not been spoken aloud in this holy place for twenty years. I look to make certain the soldier is too far away to hear. It looks like he is following that girl like she is a dog in heat. They are vile. But I shall pray.

"Praise be to Allah who created the Creation for His worship and commanded them to be just and permit the wronged one to retaliate against the oppressor in kind.

Fight in the cause of Allah those who fight you, and slay them wherever ye catch them, and turn them out from where they have turned you out; for tumult and oppression are worse than slaughter; slay them. All Praise is due to Allah."

I do not pray this properly on my knees and humbled before my Creator, for that would certainly bring the attention of the lone security guard. However, I feel very good indeed for praying here at all. I can tell nobody has the faith to slay the oppressors any longer.

Where are the people?

There is not even a television crew visiting this site. I should have liked there to be a video to commemorate the moment I slay that Jewess and the stupid guard. I pray Allah those mortar are yet waiting for me.

I see there are security cameras overlooking this square. At least I have that footage to commemorate my sacrifice. I shall be a hero of Islam, and the world will behold my valiant heart and the moment of my death.

The Muslims of this city are cowards. Infidels and hypocrites. They should all be out weeping on this holy ground in memory. Is twenty years too long? They should all be out here to watch me strike a blow for Allah, and remember the Hamas who fought here.

I know this! If our Mujahideen had but thirty minutes more than the heart of Zion would have felt the very sword of Allah! All praise to His name.

A moment of terror like never before would change the will of the world.

● ● ● ●

As if the world should change. Half way through my conversation with this guy I realize I'm an idiot. He's just an old zealot reliving the slaughter of war in his heart. Some men just love war. I wanted some kind of nostalgic camaraderie with the enemy; just like those old stories of GIs and Japanese soldiers getting together to drink tea. What a joke.

I'm getting soft. Too soft for this job.

I nod at this guy while he explains the repatriation to me. I don't buy a word. No concept of Judgment Day in Islam? Does he think I'm completely ignorant of the Qur'an?

It didn't help that I poke him in the heart about the expulsion. Still, this was something the world *HAD* to do. The terrorist forced a dragon-jinn from its bottle. The world had to react. If I did one thing right in my life it was the moment I destroyed the jinn. I defined myself as a soldier, despite my constant failures as a person. I was once a good soldier before I became so soft.

Soviet Nuclear Artillery Shell.

Dry, mind-numbing training on archaic weapons of mass destruction. My mind jumped on that boring-ass training day. Even the dust specs floating around in front of the projector came back to me. I guess the terror of the moment made my mind crystal clear.

"Really? No Qur'an text of the End of the World?" I ask this angry Muslim about his own religion. I know he is just spoon feeding me what I want to hear. For some reason he thinks it is important to lie to me about everything — even his own faith. I squint my eyes and study his hat again. It obviously cannot hold even as much as a stick. This is just a bitter guy, explaining his bitterness.

The Gunny Sergeant goes on in my head: "…After the abortive effort with purpose-built artillery pieces, the Soviet approach to nuclear artillery was that nuclear munitions should be fired by standard guns and howitzers in normal artillery units. *click slide* The first nuclear weapon for use from a standard 152 mm artillery, called ZBV3, was finally accepted in 1965. *click slide* Subsequent weapon designs followed using existing and new technology: 152 mm nuclear tipped projectile ZBV3 for self-propelled guns…"

My eyes suddenly see the artillery shell as clearly as the day I crawled along that wreckage of the buildings — long since bulldozed down to make way for this plaza.

"Well," the old Islamic believer tells me philosophically. "Islam speaks of the Judgment Day, but that is a mere metaphor."

Metaphor? Metaphor? The yield was 1 kiloton, maximum range 17.4 km when shot from a howitzer. But this was being strapped to that old-ass Hwasong-5. The fucker could carry that nuke right to Jerusalem, Tel-Aviv or anything within 300km. Even Rome I suppose.

My Gunny lectures on in my head as the Egyptian continues the song of his people: "…North Korea obtained its first Scud-Bs from Egypt in 1980. *click slide* These missiles were reverse engineered, and reproduced by North Korea as the Hwasong-5. They were exact replicas of the R-17Es obtained from Egypt. In 1985, Iran acquired 90 to 100 Hwasong missiles…"

I recognized each and every component from that speech. That dry-ass, absolutely mind-numbing, technical training session. It taught me about the devil, and here I was almost asleep during the entire talk.

Then suddenly I was looking at the very devil. Those Gunny words came back in a tumble. Those words *STILL* come to me in my sleep. I awake covered in sweat. My lovely wife just changes the bedding and washes the whole pile in the morning without a single word, or a single question. Ever. She just changes the sheets, and then snuggles right back next to me. She is the kindest thing in the world.

I say a few words to the Arab that I honestly can't remember even as I speak. My mind has traveled through some kind of time portal to the day I witnessed the end of the earth made before my eyes. I make an empty gesture to fill the present time.

"In the end it does not really matter anymore," the man returns in reply, using the same broad stroke of arm to paint an imaginary vision. "The people have forgotten and become fat and lazy. The anniversary is forgotten."

"As it should. You know that protests are prohibited today?" These words I will definitely remember because I mean. Every. Single. One. Of. Them.

I was too late to stop the first, smaller missile. Some kind of early Scud-A. I dunno maybe three meters long. It streaked away in a violent hiss. These things are fast. It was that launch that brought my attention.

I broke away from the squad and squeezed under the

collapsed rubble. I crawled my way through an entire building. I cannot honestly remember what motivated me. I hauled ass, and it still took me ten minutes to wiggle through those snatching, snagging shards of concrete.

I made it out just in time to see the Hamas and al-Qud working together to carry the nuke out on a green Islamic flag. The men shouted, '*the sword of Allah*', to the heavens.

"What's to protest? I'm just an old man sitting on a cold stone wall, remembering what this place looked like in my forgotten memory."

I glance absently at the Mujahideen.

"This place?" My voice is full of inflection for a question, but it's only because I see the past of twenty years ago. My mind is inside my younger self. The soldier fighting in the Gaza City streets that is now buried underneath the polished stones of this plaza. I am in two times at once.

I must have sounded like a crazy man as I called for an immediate Predator strike. I fought to free my laser and I painted the beast for target.

I realized there was a small chance the strike might detonate the shell instead of destroy it. Still, if I hit it before they armed the tip perhaps only a dirty fallout would stain the ground.

In worse case, I would be vaporized. In best case, just some localized radioactive contamination. I chose to hope the best, but didn't care if the worse turned me to ash. I missed the first missile, and it might be nuking an entire innocent neighborhood in Jerusalem. The Jews must retaliate, or get nuked by every Arab nation with such capability. The whole damn world would plunge into nuclear WWIII.

I lazed that bitch. Not the missile. I lazed the damned nuclear tipped ZBV3.

"Fuck that nuke!" I remember the dust puffing from the concrete as I cursed that bomb, and my life.

One of the Hamas broke away and ran off with a walkie in his hand. I suppose he was getting coordinates for the guidance system. Who knows?

At any rate, I'm tired of talking with this guy. He is just some angry, lying, old terrorist dressed in the prejudice of hating anybody who is not his exact brand of Islam.

I regret not choosing to talk to the college girl instead. Maybe I can help her figure out the path of love, and how stupid young men can be occasionally.

I say my dismissal and walk away to find where the young lady wandered off and hid.

● ● ● ●

The Will of the Fates

CHAPTER 3

A broken piece

I am still hiding away from the two old friends who share war stories. Men are sometimes boring to me. Blah… blah… this fight… blah… blah … this gun.

But what of life?

I cock my head and listen to the gusting breeze. The wind no longer carries their voices to me in the flickering air. I hear the heavy boots of the security guard making his rounds again. He should be ashamed of himself for being idle for so long.

Ah. Perhaps I am judging harshly. It is cold and there is nothing else to do. Boredom makes us do strange things.

33

Often boredom would make me search for the missile site when I otherwise would have chosen another diversion.

I would get out old satellite maps. Old ones back to when Gaza City was a refugee city and filled with so many terrorists. I can't even guess which brand of extremist killed my father. Maybe all of them?

Palestinian Islamic Jihad? Hamas? Fatah? al Nasser?

I don't know. These are just old fashioned names to me. Some of them still exists in tiny, angry knots around the world. But none of them I know intimately — that is, I do not know them since they killed my father.

I've never even seen a Hamas.

I look around for the Arab gentleman and the guard again. I do not see either of them as I measure the plaza with my strides.

From these old satellite maps I figured out where the city streets ran. I even figured out the best place for the missile launch site. The one that reached my parents had a tremendous range. Much farther than anything else shot from Gaza previously. It must have been special to these fighters. I hate it. I cannot even say out loud the model of the missile without bursting into tears. However, I know which missile that was used. I know exactly. I am not stupid.

"My brainy-snooping does make me sad sometimes. Ima is right about that." I sigh. I go back to pacing.

I would measure this courtyard with a laser ruler, but that would definitely get me arrested. I don't suppose anybody ever used a laser in this spot before.

So, there was once a building here. It was no doubt destroyed in seizing the Strip. It was a violent week until the world armies finally got control. Rumors even said there were weapons of mass destruction. Propaganda no doubt, as nothing like that was ever found.

"Six hundred and ninety-nine. Seven hundred!" I counted out loud. I am standing on the EXACT spot the missile must have launched from.

I measured the distances. I calculated the vectors. I even managed to track down the weather of that very morning to account for the wind and air density.

My father was killed with a very old Hwasong-4 missile. What some call a Scud-A.

What I do not understand is that it did not have a warhead. No explosion. It was the kinetic force alone which tore my father in half. It actually really did tear his heart out when it tore him in half. The coroner's report was very detailed. It took me almost a year of weeping too much, before I could read it all the way from beginning to end.

Perhaps the terrorists did not have a warhead? That I cannot calculate. However, I have decided that the tip must have held stones to get a perfect trajectory.

Maybe it was a test for something bigger?

I am standing on the spot. I gather my courage to say the words.

"Hwasong-4…" The tears actually leap from my eyes. I see them splash far from my feet. My lips tremble at the pain. I collapse on the spot. Right to the ground.

I am moaning in sorrow.

"Ooowww…. Oooo…" I forget the two visitors in the plaza. I am overcome with my own brainy-snooping.

Why, Oh Why am I so stupid? I knew better than provoke so tender a heart.

"I miss you." My lips still quiver and I cannot control my weeping. "I wish you would come home to me and momma. I work hard every day to make you proud… I love you…"

● ● ● ●

"I love my obedience to Allah!"

As soon as that USA-Jew soldier turned the corner behind those sheets I sprinted to the ancient olive tree.

It is strange to me that the thing survived the blast and radiation. But Allah is mysterious, and I know this was His will!

That olive tree escaped the invasion of the British, the Hitler, the Sixth American Army and the Jews. It was for this

36

very reason I chose to hide the mortars under its withered branches. I knew it would always remain despite the wars of men.

The tree alone remains of anything real from the ghosts of my memory. Every other building is gone. Bulldozed. Bombed. I run to it as if it is Paradise and I shall receive my reward.

"I am sorry my old friend," says I to the tree. "I had to run away after the Soviet Artillery shell was destroyed by the enemy. I am not a grandfather olive tree. I cannot survive the radiation."

They must have somehow swept the radiation all up. They probably put the dust in the pockets of our people when they sent us away from our holy battle ground upon Gaza.

Egyptians back to Egypt. Syrians back to Syria. Arabs back to Arabia. And so it went once the entire world took control of this tiny strip. They sent all refugees and foreigners home with filthy money in their pockets. Gaza Muslims of proof they bribed into become part of Israel if they wanted. They all wanted greedy wealth and dishonorable peace, instead of commanded Jihad! Cowards!

I shall show them all!

Yes, it was only a fragment of land, but it took the entire earth to tame our loyal Hamas — I shall even honor those other dogged soldiers who fought beside us. The Fatah was filled with idiots and reprobates. Still they helped a little, and did as well as idiots can be expected.

I grab a stone from the earth and start scratching and scraping. My eyes hardly leave my task to check for the guard. He is probably having dog-sex with that harlot. They are filthy, unclean, pigs. Vile perversion.

The tree has not grown, but my memory has changed. The first place I dig, I find nothing.

I panic believing somebody found the metal ammo crate and removed the mortars. My eyes scan the ground again in a terror. I must be a martyr!

I know I put five mortars in an Iranian ammo box myself. Twenty years ago, when Gaza City was under-seige by just the Jews and a few Americans. The world stood outside the ring, afraid to enter the fight. Paying us Gazans *AND* the Jews to fight for the world's entertainment.

I hid the mortars as I knew my leaders would negotiate a truce, and I could fire them off even before the Jews finish their retreat from the Strip.

"My own hands buried them! Why can't I find them again?" I say this aloud as a prayer to Allah.

Then Allah Himself speaks to me. He reminds me to look at the trunk of grandfather olive tree and mark the knots carefully. I smile!

"Praise be to Allah. It is the *SECOND* knot, plus seven

paces." I sprint to the knot. I calm myself and remember my stride from twenty years ago.

One. Two. Three. Four. Five. Six…Seven!

I fall to the ground in tears. I take the stone and dig and honor the names of my father and my brethren who died at the missile site. My prayers tumble in fast whispers from my trembling lips. I cannot stop my stammering tongue nor my manly tears of joy!

Clink!

I stop immediately. Nothing is more dangerous than old – very old – mortar shells. I dig quickly all around the sides, careful to avoid scratching the box.

How much time has passed? Certainly that guard should have returned by now — except he is stuck to that vile woman. Allah has made a way.

Grandfather olive tree fights me a little. His roots hold onto the box like they are his treasure. I can only remove enough soil to expose the latch. The rusty latch cuts my fingers as I rip it open.

Blood! I have already made a sacrifice of my own blood!

My eyes look inside and my heart is crushed. The devil has made the seals rotten. Water made it into the box.

I pull out each mortar carefully.

They are all ruined! Eaten away…wait. All but one. I

look closely. This one is only dirty and rusty from the others. It is still as ready to detonate as the day I put it in the sacred box. The devil has only *TRIED* to stop me. I carefully kiss this last good mortar.

This I carefully remove and in salute to my forgotten Mujahideen. I take it and I take the stone. Yes, I will hurl the stone. I will attack with old mortar and even older stone.

I saw my children dressed in green throw stones at Israeli tanks. I will hurl this stone as a symbolic memorial of their hate. How dare these interlopers dwell in any nation where Islam has been practiced. Old, or new, all infidels must worship Allah, or pay us Muslims the Jizya for their sin of disbelief.

I look about. Still the guard is off with that woman.

I kneel properly on the ground and I face my sacred Mecca. I make a long prayer of atonement and preparation of my soul to enter into paradise.

"In the Name of Allah, the Merciful, the Compassionate.

All praise is for Allah, the Lord of the Universe. May Allah bestow peace and blessings upon our Leader Muhammad, Leader of those who strive in Allah's way and Imam of the pious. May He also bestow peace and blessings upon his family and his companions, and all those who strive for the Sharee'ah until the Day of Judgment.

All Muslims Must Make Jihad

Jihad is an obligation from Allah on every Muslim and cannot be ignored nor evaded. Allah has ascribed great importance to jihad and has made the reward of the martyrs and the fighters in His way a splendid one. Only those like me who have acted similarly and who model themselves upon the martyrs of jihad can join them in this reward. Furthermore, Allah has specifically honored the Mujahideen like myself with exceptional qualities, both spiritual and practical, to benefit them in this world and the next. My pure blood is a symbol of victory in this world and the mark of success and felicity in the world to come."

I stand up.

"I will find you little Jewess." My breath exits in steam like my soul is rising already to Allah.

● ● ● ●

"There you are!" I find the girl collapsed on the marble stones. Maybe she slipped?

"Miss? Are you okay?" I ask this in my horrible Hebrew. I don't know why I bother with Hebrew.

The young lady laughs even behind her tears. She puts an embarrassed hand to her lips, and then turns to quickly wipe

41

her eyes. She is very shy.

I laugh at my Hebrew, too, despite her tears. I can tell she is not physically hurt, but merely cries over some man. I will find out who this man is that dares break this girl in half.

"No. I am fine." Her eyes drop to the ground.

Her answer is in English. I guess I will always be an American in this country. Still, her English is perfect. I smile.

"Well, I try not to pry, but I can tell you have been crying. And, as strange at this may seem, my job today is to watch over this place. I guess I could take that a step farther and say it includes the people here today."

"You mean the teeming crowd?" She quickly bites her bottom lip to silence her sassy retort.

Again, I can tell she is embarrassed by her quick wit. But, she has obviously been brought up with good manners.

"Yep. Even this teeming crowd of three. Soooo?" I look around for the old Mujahideen but can't see him behind all the shrubbery, but I do see the top of that old, old olive tree. I have no idea how that thing survived the contamination.

"I am…uh…not crying really. The cold makes my eyes to weep. I'll be better in a while." She fidgets wanting to get away. She is a crappy liar. This girl certainly lacks the cool façade of the Egyptian denizen of the frigid plaza. I kind of glance over my shoulder and see the guy has moved on. Hopefully he is going home. It's a big plaza though. He could be anywhere.

"Naw. You can't fool an old soldier like me. I'm no good with tears, but I'm pretty good at listening. You might be surprised how good it feels just to unload on a stranger. Get it out there, yanno?"

I squat down on my heels to be more personal and less threatening. I am careful to keep my jacket from displaying my side-arm. My wife doesn't really like my pistol. She accepts it as a necessary evil. What does she say? Oh yeah, '*blah...blah guns...but what about life? Why don't men talk about life?*'

I accidently chuckle aloud thinking about my wife. I realize that my small laugh makes me sound like a cold prick.

"I'm sorry. I didn't mean to chuckle just then. It's just something my wife says all the time struck me at a weird moment. '*What about life?*' she always says."

The mention of my wife makes the pretty college girl look me full in the face. Yeah, she a mess alright. Puffy eyes, swollen mottled face. Maybe eighteen or nineteen. Still, she has enough beauty that some huckster boy probably tore her heart right out.

"So what man did this to you? Made you cry like this?"

"My father." She says this without a single tear anymore. I can tell she is taking me up on my offer to '*get it all out*' and I immediately panic inside. God, I really stuck myself in it this time. I suddenly wish my wife was here. She could handle this problem. I should take my too soft-ass back out on patrol where I belong. But here goes.

"Your father?"

"He died from this very spot twenty years ago."

"Hmmm… no I don't think that is possible. You're Jewish right? Nobody Jewish died here twenty years ago. I guarantee that."

Dammit! I'm terrible at this! I should have said, *'I'm sorry'* or *'condolences'* or anything else. Instead I go right to some kind of militarily cold answer.

Condolences.

Old soldiers are never good at condolences. I don't even know why I try. I think men like me, who have killed, are cursed with some of that death forever in their own heart. It makes us dull to the earth and to love and to innocent hearts. Man, I do love my wife. Maybe that is why I love her so much. She is the innocent life that I can never be again.

But still, my sacrifice really did let her be innocent. I dunno. Life's a bitch.

"No," she corrects me as if she is my superior officer or something. "He did die from this exact spot twenty years ago. A Hwasong-4 was launched from this very spot and it tore…"

Here she goes…her voice is wavering. More sobbing in a minute. She not gonna be able to finish this sentence. But damn if this weeping girl isn't right. Those two missile are *STILL* classified to this very day. The first one was an old Scud-A. I didn't even know that at the time, but she nailed it. How could she possibly know?

She sniffs the pain away, and steadies her voice.

"...the missile came from this very place and when it hit, my father was killed. He literally lost his heart. I have lost mine every day since before I was born. So has my Ima."

The girl raises her chin. She is now a soldier of some kind. I don't know. Not like a military soldier. Still, she is a soldier because I can recognize a warrior when I see one.

Now it's my turn.

"Twenty years ago, I was stationed in a collapsed building over there." I gesture at the imaginary and forgotten building behind me.

It wasn't that Jihadist I was supposed to talk to at all. I am stunned to understand this girl was my purpose today. She and I are woven together somehow. The fates. The constellations of heaven have spoken. I am in awe at how small I am.

"The Scud that killed your father brought my attention. I hard scrambled over here, busting my as...hump."

I clear my throat. Tears drop down my face. They actually leap from my eyes and I have to deliberately steady my voice.

"Your father did not die in vain. He saved the entire world. The missile that killed him brought me to overlook the very spot you are weeping upon. You nailed it to the very millimeter. The missile came right below your feet."

"My father saved the world? He was just a professor? I don't understand. He was not fighting in Gaza."

"You can't understand. The first missile was just a test... a kind of test... I can't tell you everything. It is classified to this day. But there was another missile. Even bigger. If your father had not died, then I would not have found the second rocket... this is really important... you seem like a smart girl. Do you understand me?"

The Israeli girl tips her head. She hasn't quite found the deep, ugly, nuclear center of my carefully chosen words. I can tell her innocent heart subconsciously gets the entire thing. It's just her sweet nature forbids her to unconsciously understand my exact meaning. Hell itself lingered for a moment upon this spot twenty years ago. This innocent girl can't understand hell.

"I lazed that bitch... I put the beam on that..."

"Allahu Akbar!"

The terrorist comes shrieking around the covered shrubs with a damned mortar in one hand, and a fucken' stone in the other!

"Get back!" I scream at the girl and grab her by the hair and fling her yards behind me. Those fucken' 66mm mortars in his hand have a 66 foot kill radius. I fucken' run at the guy and try to rip my pistol from the holster.

God, I'm way too soft. Where the hell did he hide a mortar round? In his ass? It certainly wasn't under his turban or in his cloths.

I have to turn my head to look at my pistol. Can you believe I have the thing buttoned in? What kind of soldier has his gun holstered *AND* buttoned down?

Damned if that Jihadist doesn't hit me perfectly in the fucken' face with that dumb-ass stone as soon as I look away. Blood is in my eyes, but I'm still on my feet.

Fuck it. If I can't pull my pistol I sure as shit can tackle that bastard.

● ● ● ●

The Final Act

CHAPTER 4

A broken piece

Gaza has now had twenty-five years of peace to the day. Well, except for that mortar incident five years ago that was never reported in the media. Apparently, authorities felt it might illicit further attacks.

I am grateful that terrorist died in ignominy. May his name perish from the earth, to be forgotten even by God. However, I am sorry that a hero cannot be told in all his sacrifice though. I know the hero would understand. That guard didn't even flinch to run to the battle.

I bounce a pretty little girl upon my knee. She is named Maya after me, my mother and my grandmother. Tradition.

My Ima – now a real bobeshi – sits to my left. She shakes a rattle. My husband sits to my right. He is a handsome man and very good.

"Today is the anniversary of all the earth," I suddenly say.

My momma stops shaking the rattle and tears immediately fall from her eyes. I turn to my husband. I have never told him of this day. The birth of my daughter compels me to confession.

"This is bizarre, I know it," says I, "but I have the rib of a great and noble soldier embedded in my face. Right below my left eye, where all the horrible scars linger. Well, not really an entire rib. A fragment of the American GI is stuck forever in my face when he saved me from the mortar blast. The doctors say they can remove it, but I told them not to bother."

He turns his head strangely. He leans over and kisses my face. "Well, I love your scars. And so I shall love the splinter of bone in your face from the man that saved you and gave you to me and little Maya."

I nod and pat his face. He never rejected me for the scars. He doesn't even flinch at my stunning announcement.

"I lied to the doctors and claimed the pain would be too much. Actually, I like to carry around a part of that soldier, just as I carry around a piece of my father."

My pretty Ima pats my back.

My husband pours me a cup of tea.

My baby laughs upon my knee.

Strangely, a warm and gentle wind suddenly breaks the cold snap outside. You can actually hear the frosty cold dissolve into nothing from the advancing gentle, new spring air.

"Life is a beautiful thing," I say.

Shalom – The End

Stephen Paul West is an Austin Texas novelist.

If you enjoyed this work you might find the following works interesting as well:

Depression Symptoms Decoded (A Vibrant Recovery After Injury)

This self-help book is for the injured. Soldiers blasted to pieces in combat. Children crushed in bicycle accidents. People taking bone shattering falls. Victims mugged and shot. Diabetes taking a limb. Lupus taking everything.

None of these things will ever "be okay". They won't just "work themselves out." And the injured are not just magically, "gonna be all right."

This pioneering self-help book will teach you to make depression symptoms into valuable allies.
Depression will not rule you. You will rule depression.
You can totally harmonize your depression and rule it

by using the information in this work.

KWENDA – WOMEN SLAVES OF WAR

Motherhood on the point of extinction. Modern warfare has no rules, no honor, and everywhere women pay the highest costs for their children.

A woman exists always, but a mother is made only the moment her baby is born.

What would you do to save your baby in the horrors of modern war?

Prepare for a book that will move you to the core. Kwenda is a woman like no other. Carried away by endless civil wars, and bought and sold by the most powerful warlords in the world. She fights with her heart against men as hard and cold as stones. The events are real, only identities and locations have been changed to protect the innocent.

Kwenda, a captured woman of war, represents all the women torn apart in endless wars. Disobedience for them is met with horrible death.

These women are not wives, but innocent victims stolen by warlords and kept as slaves. This biographical fiction tells the harrowing tale of such a woman named "Kwenda", and has elements of every major genocide in Africa in the last 20 years from Charles Taylor to Joseph Kony and all the warlords in between.

Kwenda is a word that means Journey in several dialects. She is the voice of many women crying out as a single, powerful soul. Kwenda's life transcends all the women lost in wars to walk a single heart-breaking journey.

Lastly, in the need to protect many people, I changed names, places and created a fictional home country of Niruganya; which is an anagram of many of the countries where genocide have occurred. The reader must understand that many of these injuries are still not fully healed. If I used too accurate a brush to paint this sad story, then I might insight unnecessary violence.

The warlords were left with their names intact, so their

shame might be evident. Only the innocent were protected.

Rise of the Maiden - Blood and Venom (series)

Craving something new and sophisticated in the paranormal genre? Well, you just found it. Rise of the Maiden - Blood and Venom series will give you a glimpse into paranormal culture that you have not yet considered. Explore something fresh and new, in a genre you love!

In the first years of the reign of Victoria, a psycho kidnaps an infant girl from the dirty streets of London. For fifteen years she is held an unknowing prisoner by the captor she calls 'father'.

Based roughly on the complex secret societies that practice vampyre rites across Victorian England in the 1800's. This is a terror more real than childhood stories. It is the paranormal story reborn!